Sort It by **COLOR**

By Emmett Alexander

Gareth Stevens
PUBLISHING

first concepts

Sorting means putting things that are alike together. You can sort by color.

These toys are
different colors.

These toys are red.

These blocks are different colors.

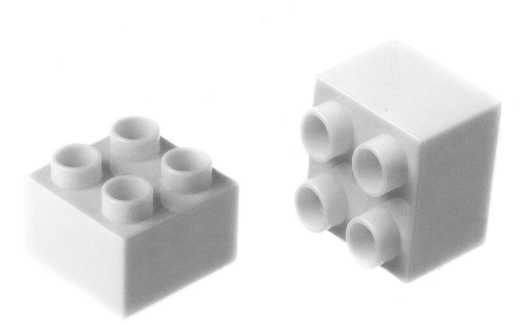

These blocks
are yellow.

These fish are
different colors.

These fish
are orange.

These vegetables are different colors.

These vegetables
are green.

These shirts are
different colors.

These shirts are blue.

13

These flowers are
different colors.

These flowers
are purple.

These crayons are different colors.

These crayons
are black.

These books are
different colors.

These books
are brown.

These rabbits are
different colors.

These rabbits
are white.

One box of balls is mixed up. How would you sort these balls by color?

Please visit our website, www.garethstevens.com. For a free color catalog of all our high-quality books, call toll free 1-800-542-2595 or fax 1-877-542-2596.

Library of Congress Cataloging-in-Publication Data

Alexander, Emmett.
Sort it by color / by Emmett Alexander.
p. cm. — (Sort it out!)
Includes index.
ISBN 978-1-4824-2565-9 (pbk.)
ISBN 978-1-4824-2566-6 (6 pack)
ISBN 978-1-4824-2567-3 (library binding)
1. Group theory — Juvenile literature. 2. Colors — Juvenile literature. I. Title.
QA174.5 A449 2016
512.2—d23

First Edition

Published in 2016 by
Gareth Stevens Publishing
111 East 14th Street, Suite 349
New York, NY 10003

Designer: Sarah Liddell
Editor: Therese Shea

Photo credits: Cover, p. 1 (polka dots) Victoria Kalinina/Shutterstock.com; cover, pp. 1 (gumballs), 23 Jenn Huls/Shutterstock.com; p. 3 Julie Vader/Shutterstock.com; pp. 4, 5 Julien Tromeur/ Shutterstock.com; p. 6 Nenov Brothers Images/Shutterstock.com; p. 7 tehcheesiong/Shutterstock.com; pp. 8, 9 Kietr/Shutterstock.com; p. 10 Serg64/Shutterstock.com; p. 11 Aprilphoto/Shutterstock.com; p. 12 GoodMood Photo/Shutterstock.com; p. 13 Apollofoto/Shutterstock.com; p. 14 Sascha Burkard/ Shutterstock.com; p. 15 Bildagentur Zoonar GmbH/Shutterstock.com; p. 16 Stephanie Frey/ Shutterstock.com; p. 17 Steve Gorton/Dorling Kindersley/Getty Images; p. 18 Quang Ho/ Shutterstock.com; p. 19 Brocreative/Shutterstock.com; p. 20 (colored rabbits) JIANG HONGYAN/ Shutterstock.com; p. 20 (white rabbit) camelia/Shutterstock.com; p. 21 (left) Eric Isselee/ Shutterstock.com; p. 21 (center) panbazil/Shutterstock.com; p. 21 (right) Iakov Filimonov/ Shutterstock.com.

Printed in the United States of America

CPSIA compliance information: Batch #CS15GS: For further information contact Gareth Stevens, New York, New York at 1-800-542-2595.